The Lieutenant of Inishmore

The Lieutenant of Inishmore

Martin McDonagh

Methuen Drama

Methuen 2001

4 6 8 10 9 7 5 3

First published in 2001 by
Methuen Publishing Limited
215 Vauxhall Bridge Road, London SW1V 1EJ

Methuen Publishing Limited Reg. No. 3543167

A CIP catalogue record for this book is availabe from the British Library

ISBN 0 413 76500 8

Typeset by SX Composing DTP, Rayleigh, Essex
Printed and bound in Great Britain by
Cox & Wyman Ltd, Reading, Berkshire

THE ROYAL SHAKESPEARE COMPANY

The Royal Shakespeare Company is probably one of the best-known theatre companies in the world. It has operated in its present form since 1961 when it changed its name from the Shakespeare Memorial Theatre Company, established a London base and widened its repertoire to embrace works other than Shakespeare.

Today the RSC has five home theatres. In Stratford the Royal Shakespeare Theatre stages large-scale productions of Shakespeare's plays; the Swan, a galleried Jacobean playhouse, brings to light the plays of many of his neglected contemporaries alongside classics of world theatre, while The Other Place, the company's studio theatre, houses some of the company's most exciting experimental and contemporary work, as well as providing a regular venue for visiting companies and some of the RSC's education work, including the annual Prince of Wales Shakespeare School.

In 1982 the company moved its London home to the Barbican Centre, where in the large-scale Barbican Theatre and the studio-sized Pit Theatre, the company stages new productions as well as the repertoire transferring from Stratford.

But Stratford and London are only part of the story. Recent years have seen a dramatic increase in the reach of the RSC, with major RSC productions on tour around the UK and abroad. Productions from Stratford and London visit regional theatres, while our annual regional tour continues to set up its own travelling auditorium in schools and community centres around the country. This ensures that the RSC's productions are available to the widest possible number of people geographically. An extensive programme of education work accompanies all this, creating the audiences of tomorrow by bringing the excitement and the power of theatre to young people all over the country. Between November 2000 and June 2001 the RSC will have presented over 40 weeks of theatre in more than 25 towns and cities in the UK, outside our own theatres.

In the past few years the company has taken Shakespeare to enthusiastic audiences in Europe, the USA, Australia and New Zealand, South America, Japan, India and Pakistan, Hong Kong, Turkey and Korea. The RSC is grateful to The British Council for its support of its overseas touring programme.

Despite enormous changes over the years, the company today continues to function very much as an ensemble of actors and actresses, whose artistic talents combine with those of the world's top directors and designers and the most highly-skilled technical teams to give a distinctive and unmistakable approach to theatre.

THE OTHER PLACE

The Other Place is the RSC's smallest theatre. The theatre also houses our rehearsal studios and has a central role in the history of the RSC as a centre for research and development.

Our roots lie in two distinct areas. In the early 1960s Michel St Denis brought to the company the European tradition of 'the actors' laboratory' and worked with actors, directors, writers, designers and technical staff to develop singly and together their own craft and imagination and that of the company.

While the company continued to explore ways of revealing Elizabethan drama, actors and directors sought new audiences for new work. Theatregoround was born. This was the first small-scale work the company had done and it laid the foundation for subsequent seasons at The Roundhouse and The Place in London. The 'tin hut' became The Other Place and Buzz Goodbody its first artistic director. In 1991 we outgrew the tin hut and moved to our present purpose-built home.

This season we celebrate our tenth anniversary in this theatre with the production of three new plays. David Edgar and Peter Whelan continue their long association with the RSC and Martin McDonagh joins them to complete our trilogy of new writing for the new century.

Since its inception The Other Place has produced work by many of the major contemporary dramatists: Edward Bond, Howard Brenton, Nick Dear, Peter Flannery, Christopher Hampton, Mike Leigh, David Rudkin, Willy Russell, Charles Wood, and more recently, Biyi Bandele, April de Angelis, Anne Devlin, Pam Gems, Robert Holman, Bernard-Marie Koltes, Derek Walcott, and Nigel Williams. This season our current exhibition in the café reflects this unique body of new writing.

Alongside these the classical balance has been maintained with new productions of European classics and Shakespeare. As well as new plays in performance, we run workshops with young writers, giving them the chance to work with RSC actors on themes which reflect the concerns of the classical repertoire.

In the present-day TOP we remember Buzz Goodbody and Michel St Denis in the rehearsal rooms named after them and their legacy continues in our developmental work. Each year we work with actors to assemble a programme of workshops focusing on different disciplines. We are members of the Union of European Theatres and RSC actors, directors and designers regularly meet their European counterparts for an exchange of ideas.

Steven Pimlott
Director of The Other Place, March 2001

THE ROYAL SHAKESPEARE COMPANY

Patron Her Majesty the Queen
President His Royal Highness The Prince of Wales
Deputy President Sir Geoffrey Cass
Chairman of the Board Lord Alexander of Weedon QC
Deputy Chairman Lady Sainsbury of Turville
Vice-Chairmen Charles Flower, Professor Stanley Wells

DIRECTION

Artistic Director Adrian Noble
Managing Director Chris Foy
Executive Producer Lynda Farran
Advisory Direction John Barton, David Brierley, Peter Brook, Terry Hands, Trevor Nunn
Emeritus Directors Trevor Nunn, Terry Hands

ASSOCIATE DIRECTORS

Michael Attenborough *Principal Associate Director*
Michael Boyd
Gregory Doran
Steven Pimlott *Director of The Other Place*

CASTING

John Cannon *Casting Director*
Ginny Schiller *Deputy Casting Director*

COMPANY MANAGEMENT

Sonja Dosanjh *Company Manager (Stratford)*
Charles Evans *Company Manager (London)*

DEVELOPMENT

Liam Fisher-Jones *Development Director*
Paula Flinders *Deputy Head of Development*

DRAMATURGY

Simon Reade *Dramaturg*
Zinnie Harris *Resident Playwright*

EDUCATION

Clare Venables *Director of Education*

FINANCE

David Fletcher *Director of Finance and Administration*
Donna Gribben *Head of Finance*
Chris O'Brien *Head of Information Technology*
Elaine Smith *Senior Management Accountant*

HUMAN RESOURCES

Rachael Whitteridge *Head of Human Resources*
Gail Miller *Health and Safety Adviser*

MARKETING

Kate Horton *Director of Marketing*
Egil Bjornsen *Sales Manager*
Andy Cole *Deputy Head of Marketing*
Kathy Elgin *Head of Publications*
Britannia Emson *Box Office Manager (London)*
Tracey Lancaster *Marketing Development Manager*
Justin Tose *Retail Manager*
Andy Williams *Acting Head of Graphics*

MUSIC

Stephen Warbeck *Head of Music & Associate Artist*
Richard Brown *Director of Music (London)*
Tony Stenson *Music Director (London)*
Michael Tubbs *Director of Music (Stratford)*
John Woolf *Music Director (Stratford)*

PLANNING

Carol Malcolmson *Planning Administrator*

PRESS AND PUBLIC AFFAIRS

Roger Mortlock *Director of Press and Public Affairs*
Katherine Hunter *Senior Press and Public Affairs Officer*

PRODUCERS

Denise Wood *Producer*

PRODUCTION

James Langley *Head of Technical Management*
Geoff Locker *Head of Production*
Simon Ash *Production Manager, Barbican Theatre*
Alan Bartlett *Head of Construction*
Charlotte Bird *Head of Production Wardrobe*
Jeremy Dunn *Stratford Sound Manager*
John Evans *Acting Head of Property Shop*
Patrick Frazer *Production Manager, The Pit Theatre*
Stuart Gibbons *Production Manager, Swan Theatre*
Mark Graham *Production Manager, The Other Place*
Brenda Leedham *Head of Wigs and Make-up*
Nigel Loomes *Head of Paint Shop*
David Parker *Production Manager RST*
Anthony Rowe *Design Co-ordinator*

SPECIAL PROJECTS

Caro MacKay *Head of Special Projects*
Jasper Gilbert *Technical Manager for Special Projects*

STRATFORD REDEVELOPMENT

Jonathan Pope *Project Director*

TECHNICAL SERVICES

Simon Bowler *Head of Technical Services*
Peter Fordham *Technical Systems (Stratford)*
David Ludlam *Technical Systems (London)*

THEATRE OPERATIONS

Caroline Felton *Director of Operations*
Neil Constable *London Manager*
Peter Cadley *Theatres Manager (London)*
Richard Rhodes *Deputy Stratford Manager*
Bronwyn Robertson *Administrator, The Other Place*
Gary Stewart *Stratford Manager*

VOICE

Andrew Wade *Head of Voice*

The RSC is incorporated under Royal Charter.
Registered Charity Number 212481

RSC EDUCATION

The objective of the RSC Education Department is to enable as many people as possible from all walks of life to have easy access to the great works of Shakespeare, the Renaissance and the theatre.

To do this, we are building a team which supports the productions that the company presents onstage for the general public, special interest groups and for education establishments of all kinds.

We are also planning to develop our contribution as a significant learning resource in the fields of Shakespeare, the Renaissance, classical and modern theatre, theatre arts and the RSC. This resource is made available in many different ways, including workshops, teachers' programmes, summer courses, a menu of activities offered to group members of the audience, pre- and post-show events as part of the Events programme, open days, tours of the theatre, community activities, youth programmes and loans of parts of the RSC Collection for exhibitions.

We are building, for use world wide, a new web site to be launched this year. The RSC will make use of the new technologies to disseminate its work in many different ways to its many audiences.

We can also use our knowledge of theatre techniques to help in other aspects of learning: classroom teaching techniques for subjects other than drama or English, including management and personnel issues.

Not all of these programmes are available all the time, and not all of them are yet in place. However, if you are interested in pursuing any of these options, or for information on general education activities, contact Education Administrator Sarah Keevill on 01789 403462, or e-mail her on sarah.keevill@rsc.org.uk.

JOIN THE RSC

For £8 a year you can become an RSC Associate Member. Benefits include:
* Advance Information and priority booking for our Stratford and London seasons (plus the RSC Residency if you live in the appropriate area).
* Special priority booking subscription scheme for the Stratford Summer Festival Season.
* Deferred payment facilities on Stratford tickets booked during the priority period (by instalments with a credit card).
* Special Members' performances for some Stratford and London productions.
* No fees payable on ticket re-sales in Stratford.
* Free RSC Magazine

Full members
For £24 all of the Associate benefits, plus:
* Guaranteed seats for RSC productions in the Royal Shakespeare Theatre, Swan Theatre and Barbican Theatre (for tickets booked during the priority period).
* An extra week of priority booking for Stratford and London seasons.
* 10% discount on purchases from RSC Shops.

Group and **Education** membership also available.

Overseas Members
The RSC tours regularly overseas. In recent years we've visited the USA, South America, Japan, India and Pakistan, as well as most parts of Europe. Wherever you are in the world, you can become an RSC Member. Overseas Membership is available from £15.

Special Overseas Members
All the benefits of a Full Member, plus:
* A complimentary programme for each Royal Shakespeare Theatre production.

For further information write to the Membership Office, Royal Shakespeare Theatre, Stratford-upon-Avon, CV37 6BB or telephone 01789 403440.

STAY IN TOUCH
For up-to-date news on the RSC, our productions and education work, visit the RSC's official web site: **www.rsc.org.uk**. Information on RSC performances is also available on Teletext.

TELETEXT
On Ch4 p430

A PARTNERSHIP WITH THE RSC

The RSC is immensely grateful for the valuable support of its corporate sponsors and individual and charitable donors. Between them these groups provide up to £6m a year for the RSC and support a range of initiatives such as actor training, education workshops and access to our performances for all members of society.

The RSC is renowned throughout the world as one of the finest arts brands. A corporate partnership offers unique and creative opportunities both nationally and internationally, and benefits from our long and distinguished record of maintaining and developing relationships. Reaching over one million theatregoers a year, our Corporate Partnership programme progresses from Corporate Membership to Business Partnership to Season Sponsor to Title Sponsor, and offers the following benefits: extensive crediting and association; prestigious corporate hospitality; marketing and promotional initiatives; corporate citizenship; and business networking opportunities. Our commitment to education, new writing and access provides a diverse portfolio of projects which offer new and exciting ways to develop partnerships which are a non-traditional and mutually beneficial.

As an individual you may wish to support the work of the RSC through membership of the RSC Patrons. For as little as £21 per month you can join a cast drawn from our audience and the worlds of theatre, film, politics and business. Alternatively, the gift of a legacy to the RSC would enable the company to maintain and increase new artistic and educational work with children and adults through the Acting and Education Funds.

For information about corporate partnership with the RSC, please contact:
Liam Fisher-Jones
Development Director
Barbican Theatre
London EC2Y 8BQ
Tel: 020 7382 7132
E-mail: liamfj@rsc.org.uk

For information about individual relationships with the RSC, please contact:
Graeme Williamson
Development Manager
Royal Shakespeare Theatre
Waterside, Stratford-upon-Avon CV37 6BB.
Tel: 01789 412661
E-mail: graemew@rsc.org.uk

You can visit our web site at **www.rsc.org.uk/development**

The Lieutenant of Inishmore was first performed by the Royal Shakespeare Company at The Other Place, Stratford-upon-Avon, on 11 April 2001. The cast was as follows:

Owen Sharpe	Davey
Trevor Cooper	Donny
David Wilmot	Padraic
Conor Moloney	James
Kerry Condon	Mairead
Colin Mace	Christy
Glenn Chapman	Joey
Stuart Goodwin	Brendan

Directed by	**Wilson Milam**
Designed by	**Francis O' Connor**
Lighting designed by	**Tim Mitchell**
Movement by	**Jonathan Butterell**
Fights by	**Terry King**
Sound by	**Matt McKenzie**
Production Manager	**Mark Graham**
Costume Supervisor	**Alastair McArthur**
Dialect Coach	**Charmian Hoare**
Company voice work by	**Charmian Hoare and Andrew Wade**

Stage Manager	**Hilary Groves** (until 9 March)
	Martin King (from 9 March)
Deputy Stage Manager	**Maddy Grant**
Assistant Stage Manager	**Lynn Howard**

To Pussy

(1981–1995)

The Lieutenant of Inishmore was first performed at the RSC, The Other Place, Stratford-upon-Avon, on 11 April 2001. The cast was as follows:

Donny	Trevor Cooper
Davey	Owen Sharpe
Padraic	David Wilmot
Mairead	Kerry Condon
James	Conor Moloney
Christy	Colin Mace
Brendan	Stuart Goodwin
Joey	Glenn Chapman

Director Wilson Milam
Designer Francis O'Connor
Lighting Designer Tim Mitchell
Sound Matt McKenzie

Characters

Donny, *mid-forties. Padraic's father. From Inishmore.*
Davey, *seventeen. Slightly overweight, long hair. From Inishmore.*
Padraic, *twenty-one. Handsome. From Inishmore.*
Mairead, *sixteen. Cropped hair, pretty. Davey's sister. From Inishmore.*
James, *twenties / thirties. Northern Irish.*
Christy, *thirties / forties. Northern Irish.*
Brendan, *twenty. Northern Irish.*
Joey, *twenty. Northern Irish.*

The play is set in 1993 on the island of Inishmore, County Galway.

Scene One

A cottage on Inishmore circa 1993. Front door in centre of back wall, a window to its left and right. Exit stage left to a bathroom, unseen, an open area forward right to signify another room. A clock somewhere on back wall along with a framed piece of embroidery reading 'Home Sweet Home'. Cupboards left and right, a telephone on one of them. A couple of armchairs near the back wall and a table centre, on which, as the play begins, lies a dead black cat, its head half missing. **Donny**, *the middle-aged owner of the house, and* **Davey**, *a long-haired, slightly pudgy neighbour of seventeen, stand staring quietly at this cat for a few moments.*

Davey   Do you think he's dead, Donny?

Pause. **Donny** *picks up the limp dead cat. Bits of its brain plop out.* **Donny** *looks across at* **Davey** *and puts the cat back down again.*

Donny   Aye.

Davey   He might be in a coma. Would we ring the vet?

Donny   It's more than a vet this poor feck needs.

Davey   If he gave him an injection?

Donny (*pause*)   Have this injection, you!

Donny *steps back and kicks* **Davey** *up the arse.*

Davey (*almost crying*)   What was that fer?!

Donny   How many times have people told you, hairing down that bastarding hill on that bastarding bicycle?

Davey   I didn't touch the poor fella, I swear it! In the road I saw him lying . . . !

Donny   In the road me arsehole!

Davey   And I wasn't hairing at all, I was going slow. And a black lump ahead in the road I saw, and what the devil's that, I said to meself . . .

Donny   After you'd rode over him, aye, and then probably reversed!

Davey   Ahead in the road, I'm saying, and don't be slinging reversed at me.

Donny   I'll be slinging what I like!

Davey   And I was off me bike be that time anyway and just wheeling it along, and when I saw it was Wee Thomas didn't I scoop him up and run him into you as quick as me legs could carry me?

Donny   The first thing the books say is don't be moving an accident victim till professional fecking help arrives, and a fool knows that!

Davey   Well, I don't be reading books on cats being knocked down, Donny!

Donny   Well, maybe you should, now . . .

Davey   Because there *are* no such books!

Donny   . . . And maybe Thomas would still be with us then.

Davey   A car it must have been clobbered him.

Donny   No cars have been down that road all day, and when do cars ever come down that road? You're the only bastard comes down that lonely road and why? Because you're a cowshite eejit with nothing better to do than roar down roads on your mam's bicycle for no reason other than to feel the wind in that girl's mop o' hair of yours!

Davey   If you're insulting me hair again, Donny Osbourne, I'll be off right this minute. After going out of me way to bring your cat in to you . . .

Donny   After squashing the life out of me cat, and he isn't my cat at all . . .

Davey   So as not to let the oul flies be picking the meat off him. A favour I was doing you.

Donny   It's a favour now! With half of that cat's head poking out of the spokes of your wheels, I'll bet, and it's a favour you're doing me!

Davey *stares at* **Donny** *a moment, then darts out through the front door.* **Donny** *goes over to the cat and strokes it sadly, then sits in the armchair stage left, looking at the cat's blood on his hands.* **Davey** *returns a few moments later, dragging his mum's bicycle in through the door. It is pink, with small wheels and a basket. He brings it right over for* **Donny** *to see, raises its front wheel so that it's almost in* **Donny**'*s face, and starts slowly spinning it.*

Davey   Now where's your cat's head? Eh? Now where's your cat's head?

Donny (*depressed*)   Scraping it off on the way wouldn't have been a hard job.

Davey   There's no cat's head on that bicycle wheel. Not even a stain, nor the comrade of a stain, and the state of Wee Tommy you'd have had lumps of brain pure dribbling.

Donny   Put your bicycle out of me face, now, Davey.

Davey   Poor Wee Thomas's head, a bicycle wouldn't do damage that decent. Damage that decent you'd have to go out of your way to do.

Donny   Your bicycle out of me face, I'm saying, or it'll be to your head there'll be decent damage done.

Davey *leaves the bike at the front door.*

Davey   Either a car or a big stone or a dog you'd need to do that decent damage. And you'd hear a dog.

Donny   And you'd hear a car.

Davey (*pause*)   You'd probably hear a big stone too. It depends on how big and from what distance. Poor Wee Thomas. I did like him, I did. Which is more than I can say for most of the cats round here. Most of the cats round here I wouldn't give a penny for. They're all full of themselves. Like our Mairead's cat. You'd give him a pat, he'd outright sneer. But Wee Thomas was a friendly cat. He would always say hello to you were you to see him sitting on a wall. (*Pause.*) He won't be saying hello no more, God bless him. Not with that lump of brain gone. (*Pause.*) And you haven't had him long at all, have you, Donny? Wasn't he near brand new?

Donny   He isn't my fecking cat at all is what the point of the fecking matter is, and you know full well.

Davey   I don't know full well. What . . . ?

Donny   Only fecking looking after the bastard I was the year.

Davey   Who were you fecking looking after him for, Donny?

Donny   Who do you think?

Davey (*pause*)   Not . . . not . . .

Donny   Not what?

Davey (*with horror*)   Not your . . . not your . . .

Donny   Aye.

Davey   No!

Donny   Why else would I be upset? I don't get upset over cats!

Davey   Not your Padraic?!

Donny   Aye, my Padraic.

Davey   Oh Jesus Christ, Donny! Not your Padraic in the INLA?!

Donny   Do I have another fecking Padraic?

Davey   Wee Thomas is his?

Donny   And was his since he was five years old. His only friend for fifteen year. Brought him out to me when he started moving about the country bombing places and couldn't look after him as decent as he thought needed. His only friend in the world, now.

Davey   Was he fond of him?

Donny   Of course he was fond of him.

Davey   Oh he'll be mad.

Donny   He *will* be mad.

Davey   As if he wasn't mad enough already. Padraic's mad enough for seven people. Don't they call him 'Mad Padraic'?

Donny   They do.

Davey   Isn't it him the IRA wouldn't let in because he was *too* mad?

Donny   It was. And he never forgave them for it.

Davey   Maybe he's calmed down since he's been travelling.

Donny   They tell me he's gotten worse. I can just see his face after he hears. And I can just see your face too, after he hears your fault it was. I can see him plugging holes in it with a stick.

Davey (*dropping to his knees*)   Oh please, Donny, I swear to God it wasn't me. Don't be saying my name to him, now. Sure, Padraic would kill you for sweating near him, let alone this. Didn't he outright cripple the poor fella laughed at that girly scarf he used to wear, and that was when he was twelve?!

Donny   His first cousin too, that fella was, never minding twelve! And then pinched his wheelchair!

Davey   Please now, Donny, you won't be mentioning my name to him?

Donny *gets up and ambles around.* **Davey** *stands also.*

Donny   If you admit it was you knocked poor Thomas down, Davey, I won't tell him. If you carry on that it wasn't, then I will. Them are your choices.

Davey   But it isn't fecking fair, Donny!

Donny   I don't know if it is or it isn't.

Davey   I knew well I should've up and ignored the bastard when I saw him lying there, for if a black cat crossing your path is bad luck, what must one of the feckers lying dead in front of you be? Worse luck. I killed Wee Thomas so, if that's what you want to hear.

Donny   How?

Davey   How? However you fecking want, sure! I hit him with me bike, then I banged him with a hoe, then I jumped up and down on the feck!

Donny   You hit him with your bike, uh-huh, I suspected. But an accident it was?

Davey   An accident, aye. A pure fecking accident.

Donny   Well . . . fair enough if an accident is all it was.

Davey (*pause*)   So you won't be mentioning my name so?

Donny   I won't be.

Davey   Good-oh. (*Pause.*) When'll you be informing him of the news?

Donny   I'll give him a ring in a minute now. He has a mobile.

Davey   He'll be furious.

Donny   I'll tell him . . . I'll tell him Wee Thomas is poorly, I'll tell him. Aye . . .

Davey   Sure he'll know he's more than poorly, Donny, when he sees them brains bubbling away . . .

Donny   He's poorly but there's no need to be *rushing home*, I'm saying . . .

Davey   I'm with you now, Donny . . .

Donny   Do you get me? He's just a tadeen off his food, like, I'll tell him. And in a week I'll say he's going downhill a biteen. And in another week I'll say he passed away peaceful in his sleep, like.

Davey   You'll be letting him down easy.

Donny   I'll be letting him down easy.

Davey   You won't give him the bad news all at once. You'll do it in stages, like.

Donny   The last thing we want is Padraic roaring home to a dead cat, now.

Davey   Oh Donny, that's the last thing in the world you'd want.

Donny   That's the last thing *you'd* want too. You're the bastard brained him, you've admitted.

Davey *goes to say something but doesn't, just squirms.*

Donny   Eh?

Davey   Aye, aye, I am the bastard . . . (*mumbling*) for feck's sake . . .

Donny   I'll give him a ring now, I will.

Davey (*mumbling*)   Give him a ring now, for your fecking self, aye, ya feck.

Donny *stands there biting his bottom lip.* **Davey** *goes to the door and picks up his bike.*

Davey   Drove on a-fecking-head I should've, I knew! I'm too kind to little things is my fecking trouble!

Donny *picks up the telephone, staring at the cat.*

Donny   Oh Wee Tommy, you poor beggar. As fecked up as you are, it mightn't be long till we're just as fecked up as you if that lube turns up. Just as fecked up? Twice as fecked up is more like.

Davey   Three times as fecked up probably, Donny, or maybe four times?

Donny   Be fecking off home you, ya cat brainer.

Davey   I will. And I'll be braining some more cats on me way home, cos it's me fecking hobby now, so it is.

Donny (*absently*)   Don't be braining any more cats, now.

Davey *sighs, rolls his eyes to the ceiling and wheels his bike out.*
Donny *starts dialling a number slowly, sadly. Fade to black.*

Scene Two

A desolate Northern Ireland warehouse or some such. **James**, *a bare-chested, bloody and bruised man, hangs upside down from the ceiling, his feet bare and bloody.* **Padraic** *idles near him, wielding a cut-throat razor, his hands bloody. Around* **Padraic**'s *chest are strapped two empty holsters and there are two handguns on a table stage left.* **James** *is crying.*

Padraic   James? (*Pause.*) James?

James (*sobbing*)   Wha'?

Padraic   Do you know what's next on the agenda?

James   I don't. And I don't want to know.

Padraic   I know well you don't, you big feck. Look at the state of you, off bawling like some fool of a girl.

James   Is a fella not supposed to bawl so, you take his fecking toenails off him?

Padraic (*pause*)   Don't be saying 'feck' to me, James . . .

James   I'm sorry, Padraic . . .

Padraic   Or you'll make me want to give you some serious bother, and not just be tinkering with you.

James   Is toenails off just tinkering with me, so?

Padraic   It is.

James   Oh, it's just fecking tinkering with me toenails off is . . .

Padraic   James Hanley, don't keep going on about your stupid fecking toenails! The way you talk it sounds as if I took off a rake of them, when it was only two I took off, and them only small ones. If they'd been big ones I could understand, but they weren't. They were small. You'd hardly notice them gone. And if it was so concerned you were about the health of them toenails it would've been once in a while you cleaned out the muck from under them.

James   Well, you've saved me that job for good now anyways.

Padraic   If I hadn't been such a nice fella I would've taken one toenail off of separate feet, but I didn't, I took two toenails off the one foot, so that it's only the one foot you'll have to be limping on and not the two. If it had been the two you'd've found it a devil to be getting about. But with the pain concentrated on the one, if you can get hold of a crutch or a decent stick, I'm not sure if the General Hospital does hand them out but they might do, I don't know. You could phone them up and ask, or go in and see them would be the best thing, and make sure them toes won't be going septic at the same time. I didn't disinfect this razor at all, I never do, I see no need, but they'd be the best people to ask, sure they're the experts. You'll probably need a tetanus jab too, oh there's no question. I do hate injections, I do. I think I'd rather be slashed with a razor than have an injection. I don't know why. Of course, I'd rather have neither. You'll have had both by the end of the day. What a bad day you've had. (*Pause.*) But, em . . . I have lost me train of thought now, so I have.

James   You've lost your train of thought? Uh-huh. As slow as that fecking train is, and you've lost it?

Padraic (*pause*)   The next item on the agenda is which nipple of yours do you want to be saying goodbye to. The right or the left?

James   No, now. Come on, now . . . !

Padraic   Be picking, I'm saying! Whichever's your favourite nipple I won't be touching that fella at all, I'll be concentrating on the other. I'll be giving him a nice sliceen and then probably be feeding him to ya, but if you don't pick and pick quick it'll be both of the boys you'll be waving goodbye to, and waving goodbye to two tits when there's no need but to wave goodbye to one makes no sense at all as far as I can see. In *my* eyes, like. In fact it's the mark of a madman. So be picking your nipple and we'll get the ball rolling, for I have better things to do with me time than to be hanging around warehouses cutting *your* nipples off, James Hanley.

James (*crying*)   But I've done nothing at all to deserve nipples off, Padraic!

Padraic   Oh, let's not be getting into the whys and wherefores, James. You do push your filthy drugs on the schoolchildren of Ireland, and if you concentrated exclusive on the Protestants I'd say all well and good, but you don't, you take all comers.

James   Marijuana to the students at the Tech I sell, and at fair rates . . . !

Padraic   Keeping our youngsters in a drugged-up and idle haze, when it's out on the streets pegging bottles at coppers they should be.

James   Sure, everybody smokes marijuana nowadays.

Padraic   I don't!

James   Well, maybe you should! It might calm you down!

Padraic   Be picking your nipple, I'm saying!

James   Paul McCartney says it should be outright legalised! He says it's less bad than booze and it cures epileptics!

Padraic   Say goodbye to them both so.

James   He has statistics, Padraic!

Padraic *approaches him quickly with the razor.*

James   The right one! The right one!

Padraic *takes* **James***'s right tit in his hand so that the nipple points out, and is just about to slice it off . . .*

Padraic   Grit your teeth, James. This may hurt.

James (*screaming*)   No . . . !

. . . when the cellphone in **Padraic***'s back pocket rings loudly.*

Padraic   Will you hang on there a minute, James . . . ?

Padraic *answers the phone, idling away from* **James***, who is left shaking and whimpering behind him.*

(*Into phone.*) Hello? Dad, ya bastard, how are you? (*To* **James**.) It's me dad. (*Pause.*) I'm grand indeed, Dad, grand. How is all on Inishmore? Good-oh, good-oh. I'm at work at the moment, Dad, was it important now? I'm torturing one of them fellas pushes drugs on wee kids, but I can't say too much over the phone, like . . .

James (*crying*)   *Marijuana*, Padraic.

Padraic   They *are* terrible men, and it's like they don't even know they are, when they know well. They think they're doing the world a favour, now. (*Pause.*) I haven't been up to much else, really. I put bombs in a couple of chip shops, but they didn't go off. (*Pause.*) Because chip shops aren't as well guarded as army barracks. Do I need your advice on planting bombs? (*Pause.*) I was pissed off, anyways. The fella who makes our bombs, he's fecking useless. I think he does drink. Either they go off before you're ready or they don't go off at all. One thing about the IRA anyways, as much as I hate the bastards, you've got to hand it to them, they know how to make a decent bomb. (*Pause.*) Sure, why would the IRA be selling us any of their bombs? They need them themselves, sure. Those bastards'd charge the earth anyways. I'll tell ya, I'm getting pissed off with the whole thing. I've been thinking of forming a splinter group. (*Pause.*) I know we're already a splinter group, but there's no law says you can't splinter from a splinter group. A splinter group is the best kind of group to splinter from anyways. It shows you know your own mind (*Whispering.*), but there's someone in the room, Dad, I can't be talking about splinter groups. (*To* **James**, *politely.*) I'll be with you in a minute now, James.

James *shudders slightly.*

Padraic　What was it you were ringing about anyways, Dad?

Pause. **Padraic**'s *face suddenly becomes very serious, eyes filling with tears.*

Eh? What about Wee Thomas? (*Pause.*) Poorly? How poorly, have you brought him to the doctor? (*Pause.*) *How* long has he been off his food, and why didn't you tell me when it first started? (*Pause.*) He's not too bad? Either he's poorly or he's not too bad now, Dad, he's either one or the fecking other, there's a major difference, now, between not too bad and fecking poorly, he cannot be the fecking two at fecking once, now, (*Crying heavily.*) and you wouldn't be fecking calling me at all if he was not too bad, now! What have you done to Wee Thomas now, you fecking bastard? Put Wee Thomas on the phone. He's sleeping? Well, put a blanket on him and be stroking and stroking him and get a second opinion from the doctor and don't be talking loud near him and I'll be home the first fecking boat in the fecking morning. Ar, you fecker, ya!

Padraic *smashes the phone to pieces on the table, shoots the pieces a few times, then sits there crying quietly. Pause.*

James   Is anything the matter, Padraic?

Padraic   Me cat's poorly, James. Me best friend in the world, he is.

James   What's wrong with him?

Padraic   I don't know, now. He's off his food, like.

James   Sure that's nothing to go crying over, being off his food. He probably has ringworm.

Padraic   Ringworm? Is that serious, now?

James   Sure, ringworm isn't serious at all. Just get him some ringworm pellets from the chemist and feed them him wrapped up in a bit of cheese. They don't like the taste of ringworm pellets, cats, so if you hide them in a bit of cheese he'll eat them unbeknownst and never know the differ, and he'll be as right as rain in a day or two, or at the outside three. Just don't exceed the stated dose. Y'know, read the instructions, like.

Padraic   How do you know so much about ringworm?

James   Sure, don't I have a cat of me own I love with all my heart, had ringworm a month back?

Padraic   Do ya? I didn't know drug pushers had cats.

James   Sure, drug pushers are the same as anybody underneath.

Padraic   What's his name?

James   Eh?

Padraic   What's his name?

James   Em, Dominic. (*Pause.*) And I promise not to sell drugs to children any more, Padraic. On Dominic's life I promise. And that's a big promise, because Dominic means more to me than anything.

Padraic (*pause*)   Are you gipping me now, James?

James   I'm not gipping you. This is a serious subject.

Padraic *approaches* **James** *with the razor and slices through the ropes that bind him.* **James** *falls to the floor in a heap, then half picks himself up, testing out his weight on his bloody foot.* **Padraic** *holsters his guns.*

Padraic   How are them toes?

James   They're perfect, Padraic.

Padraic   You admit you deserved the toes at least?

James   Oh I did. The toes and an arm, really.

Padraic   Do you have money to get the bus to the hospital?

James   I don't.

Padraic *gives the confused* **James** *some change.*

Padraic   Because you want to get them toes looked at. The last thing you want now is septic toes.

James   Oh d'you know, that's the last thing I'd want.

Padraic   I'm off to Galway to see me cat.

Padraic *exits.*

James (*calling out*)   And I hope by the time you get home he's laughing and smiling and as fit as a fiddle, Padraic!

Pause. Sound of a distant outer door banging shut.

(*Crying.*)   I hope that he's dead already and buried in shite, you stupid mental fecking bastard, ya!

Blackout.

Scene Three

A country lane. **Davey** *has his bike propped upside down and is lovingly pumping up its tyres. Distinctive whizzing shots from an air rifle begin to sound, one of them hitting* **Davey** *in the cheek, making him dive down behind his bike, the others bouncing off the bike itself.*

Davey   Ar, ya fecker, Mairead! Ya big fecker, you! You got me in the cheek there!

The shooting stops, **Davey** *whimpering.*

Mairead (*off*)   In the cheek, is it?

Davey   You could've had me fecking eye out!

Mairead (*entering*)   That was the object, to have your fecking eye out. I've failed now.

Mairead *is a girl of sixteen or so, slim, pretty, with close-cropped hair, army trousers, white T-shirt, sunglasses. She carries an air rifle and starts kicking* **Davey**'s *bicycle into the ditch as he gets up, examining his bloody cheek.*

Davey   Leave me fecking bike alone, now! Is it not enough you shoot me in the face, let alone battering me bicycle on top of it?

Mairead   No, it's not enough! It's not enough at all for your crimes!

Davey   What fecking crimes, ya lube?! Leave me fecking bike, now!

He shoves **Mairead** *away from the bike. She falls to the ground, then slowly picks herself up, cocks her gun and aims it at* **Davey**'s *face.*

(*Hands raised.*) I didn't mean to push you that hard, Mairead, I promise. *Don't*, now! I'll be telling Mam on ya!

Mairead   Go ahead and tell Mam, only you'll have to tell her with no eyes!

Davey   What's got into your mad head at all?

Mairead   The poor cat you rammed to skitter this morning is what's got into my mad head at all.

Davey   Ah, feck, I rammed no cat at all! How did you hear that story?

Mairead   The news it was on.

Davey   It was on no news, and when do you ever watch the news unless there's been a bomb in England gone off you can laugh o'er?

Mairead   A little bird did tell me, so.

Davey   Well, if he told you I did anything other than ride along slow and see a dead cat in the road and pick it up gentle and run it into Donny's then that little bird is a dirty fecking liar and I'll say it to that bird's fecking face. (*Pause.*) That was the entire of it, Mairead. Sure, I have as much concern for the cats of this world as you do, only I don't go around saying it, because if I went around saying it they'd call me an outright gayboy, and they do enough of that with me hairstyle.

Mairead *lowers the gun and idles around.*

Davey   You'd have blinded your brother over a dead cat.

Mairead   I would. Without a question.

Davey   And then you say you're not mad.

Mairead   I'm not at all mad.

Davey   I could round up ten cows with only one eye would disagree.

Mairead   Don't keep bringing them cows' eyes up! Them cows' eyes was a political protest!

Davey   Against cows? Sure, what have cows done?

Mairead   Against the fecking meat trade, and you know well!

Davey   I can't see how shooting cows in the eyes is going to do any damage to the meat trade, now.

Mairead   Of course you can't, because you're a thick. Don't you know that if you take the profit out of the meat trade it'll collapse in on itself entirely, and there's no profit at all in taking ten blind cows to market, I'll tell ya. There's a loss. For who would want to buy a blind cow?

Davey   No one.

Mairead   No one is right. So in those circumstances I did see cows as valid targets, though my thinking has gone full tilt since then, and they are valid targets no longer.

Davey   Aye. It's only wee lads and their bicycles you see as valid targets nowadays.

Mairead   If they're suspected of doing damage to cats it is, aye.

Davey   Well, I was doing no damage to that cat. I was trying to help that cat, and help Donny too, and amn't I still trying to help Donny, running arse-faced errands I'm a dead man if I fail in.

Mairead   What errands?

Davey   He's got me roaming the country to find a black cat identical to his Wee Thomas, so that when Padraic roars home at high noon tomorrow it won't be a cat with a half a head we'll be placing in his arms.

Mairead   Sure, do you think Padraic's thick?

Davey   What we're banking on is that Padraic's as thick as a mongo fecking halfwit.

Mairead *pokes his bloody cheek.*

Mairead   Don't be saying mongo halfwit about a brave son of Erin, now, David!

Davey   I won't be, Mairead.

Mairead   Padraic'll be able to tell the differ straight off between a cat that's his and a cat that isn't. Sure, isn't he a second-lieutenant at the age of twenty-one, sure?

Davey   He is, aye, a second-lieutenant. In his own brain if nowhere else.

Mairead   Sure, every cat has its own separate personality, sure, not to mention its eyes and its miaow. Look at my Sir Roger. Sir Roger has a different personality to any cat. Any cat I've ever known, anyways . . .

Davey   Aye. He's a snooty little bitch.

Mairead   He's no snooty little bitch.

Davey   He's a snooty bitch and he tore two of me *X-men* comics the other day and on purpose . . .

Mairead   Good on Sir Roger, so.

Davey   So don't be defending him.

Mairead   I will do what I wish.

Davey   Is me cheek still bleeding?

Mairead   It is.

Davey (*quietly*)   Ya feck.

Davey *sets up his bike again and starts pumping it as before.*
Mairead *idles, swinging her gun around her fingers and singing 'The Dying Rebel'.*

Mairead (*singing*)   'The last I met was a dying rebel . . .'

Davey   Ar, don't be singing your fool fecking rebel songs again, now, Mairead!

Mairead (*singing*)   'Kneeling low I heard him say, God bless my home in dear Cork City, God bless the cause for which I die.'

Davey (*singing over her last line – Motorhead*)   'The ace of spades! The ace of spades!'

Christy, *Northern Irish, in a dark suit, sporting an eyepatch, enters right, walking along the road. He stops as he's about to pass the two.*

Christy   Howdo?

Davey   Howdo?

Christy   That's a nice wee gun.

Mairead   It gets the job done.

Christy (*to* **Davey**)   I've seen you somewhere before, I'm thinking.

Davey   I don't know if you have or you haven't.

Christy   Today, even, it may've been. I remember your girly hair.

Davey *tuts.*

Christy   Weren't you the fella I saw rode over the cat on the road this morning?

Davey   I rid over no cat!

Mairead *backs off, stern-faced, sits on a rock stage left and stares at* **Davey** *throughout.* **Davey** *is aware of this, nervous.*

Christy   Did you not, now? I must be mistaken, so.

Davey   I rode *up to* a cat, slow, and when I saw he was in a bad way I ran him into the fella he belongs to to try and save him, as fast as me legs could carry me.

Christy   The fella whose he is must've been upset.

Davey   He *was* upset. And the cat isn't even his either. It's another fella's.

Christy   Is that fella upset?

Davey   He will be tomorrow when he gets home. He thinks it's only poorly. It isn't poorly. It's buried in his potatoes.

Christy   Uh-huh. What time will this other fella be home?

Davey   Uh . . . twelve, I think. Aye, twelve.

Christy *nods and begins to walk off stage left.*

Christy   All the best to yous.

Davey   Fella? Will you tell me sister you were wrong when you said I rid over that cat? Isn't it right you only saw me ride up to it, slow, like, if anything at all you saw?

Christy (*pause*)   I was brought up be Jesuits. And the thing the Jesuits tell you, 'It's a terrible thing to go lying.' Of course, a fella's eyes can often play tricks on him, especially when he only has one eye, but as sure as shite I'd swear you aimed for that cat's head full-pelt, then near enough reversed on the fecker. I'll be seeing you.

Christy *exits stage left.* **Mairead** *cocks her rifle.*

Davey   I did no such . . .

Davey *sprints off stage right, covering his face as he goes.* **Mairead** *shoots after him, then kicks his bicycle over and starts shooting at it. Slow fade to black.*

Mairead   And only the fecking start this is, Davey Claven! You'll be dead as that cat be the time this is over, if not more dead, ya feck, ya!

Scene Four

Night. **Donny**'s *house.* **Donny** *is standing, swigging poteen from the bottle, his hands black, watching* **Davey** *trying to cover a ginger cat in black shoe polish and doing a very poor job of it. Both men are very drunk.*

Donny   He'll suspect.

Davey   He won't.

Donny (*pause*)   He will, now.

Davey   I amn't half finished yet. Don't be criticising until you've seen the finished job now, Donny.

Donny *staggers to the armchair left and sits, taking another swig.*

Davey   And don't be hogging that poteen.

Donny   It is my poteen to hog.

Davey *goes over and takes a swig himself, then continues on the cat.*

Donny   As soon as he walks through the door he'll know that isn't his cat. Sure that cat's orange.

Davey   He won't be orange by the time I've finished with the feck. He'll be black as a coon.

Donny   You should've got a black cat at the outset, never minding coons.

Davey *waves the cat in the air.*

Davey   If you don't like the cat I got you then I'll take the fecker and go. We didn't come here to be criticised.

Donny   Stay and be finishing, ya long-haired goob. Be putting some on his gob, there. He's pure orange on his gob.

Davey (*continuing painting the cat*)   Five mile I roamed looking for a black cat, and walking, after me bitch sister bashed up me bicycle, and no black cats was there, or if there was they was being played with be children, and I am no man to be pinching cats off of children.

Donny   Aye. No guts for the job. I knew well.

Davey   It isn't guts at all. It's having enough of a heart not to make poor gasurs go crying. (*Mumbled.*) And their mams were there anyways.

Donny   I'll bet their mams were there. And if you were any kind of a man at all you'd've walked up to them mams and said 'I'm taking yere kids' cat', and if they'd put up a show you could've given them a belt, and then trampled on the bitches!

Davey   I'm no man to go trampling on mams. Not for the sake of a cat anyways. Would you've liked your mam trampled on when she was alive?

Donny   Many's the time I trampled on my mam when she was alive. After she'd died I stopped. There seemed no sense.

Davey   What did you go trampling on your mam for?

Donny   Ah, she'd get on me nerves.

Davey   I can see where your Padraic does get his outlook on life now.

Donny   That awful, hairy chin on her. (*Pause.*) Let me have a crack at that cat, now. You do a poor job of cat covering.

Donny *gets up and* **Davey** *lets him take over, sitting down with the poteen.*

Davey   I was trying to make the polish go further. There's hardly a smatter left.

Donny   If you knew it was an orange cat you were bringing you should've brought your own shoe polish, and not go skittering away mine.

Davey   Is it orders you're pegging me now?

Donny   You should've come prepared. This cat's going to end up only half black, and if he goes licking himself in the night on top of it, the jig'll truly be up, boy.

Davey (*pause*)   Cats are forever licking themselves. I don't know why. More than dogs. It must be something in their brains. Aye.

Donny (*funny voice*)   I am putting some on your head now, baby, be closing your eyes so they will not be stinging and you would go crying.

Davey   That cat's an awful cry-baby.

Donny   Where did you get this cat?

Davey   Ah, just off somebody.

Donny   It does have a tag. What's its name, now . . . ?

Davey   Sir Roger.

Donny   Sir Roger. That's a funny name for a cat.

Davey   It is. It was probably some mental case named that cat.

Donny   Will I take his name tag off, Davey? Else that'd give the game away straight off.

Davey   Take it off, aye, else Padraic'd be reading it and know straight off by the name it wasn't Wee Thomas. That was intelligent thinking, Donny.

Donny   I know well it was. I don't need your opinion on my intelligencientiousness.

Donny *tosses the name tag on to a cupboard left.*

Davey (*pause*)   We could tell him Wee Thomas has a disease makes him go orangey-looking.

Donny   We could, d'you know?

Davey   And smell of shoe polish.

Donny   Do you think that'd work, Davey?

Davey   No.

Donny   What did you fecking say it for, so?

Davey   Just for the sake of it, Donny.

Donny *tuts.*

Davey   Was that true, Donny, about you trampling on your mam, now?

Donny (*smiling*)   I was exaggerating a biteen.

Davey   I was thinking.

Donny   I did kick her once but that was all I did.

Davey　I was thinking. Your mam'd have to have done something awful wrong for you to go trampling on her. I love my mam. Love her more than anything. Love her more than anything.

Donny *is almost running out of shoe polish. The cat is less than half covered, looking completely ridiculous.*

Davey　Mm. I do like the smell of shoe polish, I do.

Donny　The same as that, I do.

The two of them sniff their black hands deeply.

It does make you want to eat it.

Davey　It does. Have you ever tried it?

Donny　When I was young.

Davey　The same as that. Isn't it coarse?

Donny　It is. And they know what you've been doing be the state of your tongue.

Davey　And then they laugh at you.

Donny　Aye. (*Pause.*) There we go, now . . .

He finishes polishing the cat, then holds him up high in the air for **Davey** *to see.*

What do you think, Davey? Will we get away with it?

Davey *considers for a few moments.*

Davey　He'll put a gun to our heads and blow out what little brains we have.

Donny (*laughing*)　He will!

Blackout.

Scene Five

Roadside. Night. **Christy**, **Brendan** *and* **Joey**, *who sits apart from the other two.* **Christy** *eats beans from a can. All have Northern Irish accents.*

Christy   Come over and eat some beans, you.

Joey   I don't eat beans with fellas the likes of ye.

Brendan   The babby's going crying now.

Joey   I'm not going crying either.

Christy   Don't start arguing again, you two.

Brendan   Shitting his knickers at the job he has in hand.

Joey   Shitting me knickers? Do you want to see me knickers to see if they're shitted?

Brendan   I don't!

Joey   No shit is there at all in my knickers. I've the balls to take on any feck. No matter how big or grand. But what I don't have, I don't have to go out of me way to pick on wee fellas I'm twenty times bigger than and who are unarmed, and who never will be armed because they have no arms. Just paws.

Christy   We none of us enjoyed today's business, Joey-o, but hasn't the plan worked? And like the fella said, 'Don't the ends justify the means?' Wasn't it Marx said that, now? I think it was.

Brendan   It wasn't Marx, no.

Christy   Who was it then?

Brendan   I don't know, now. It wasn't Marx is all I'm saying.

Christy   Oh, Brendan, you're always cutting people down and saying who didn't say things. A fool can say who didn't say things. It takes intelligence to put your neck on the line and say who did say things.

Brendan   I suppose it does, but it wasn't Marx, is all I'm saying.

Christy   So who was it then?

Brendan   I don't know!

Christy   It was some feck to do with Russia!

Brendan   It may have been, and it probably was. It sounds like something them fecks would say. What I'm saying, Christy, it wasn't fecking Marx, now!

Christy   There's no talking to this fella.

Brendan   Not on the subject of quotes, no.

Joey (*pause*)   Ye've changed the subject on me.

Christy   What was the subject?

Joey   Battering in the head of an innocent cat was the subject! I don't remember agreeing to batter cats when I joined the INLA.

Brendan   What cat did you batter? Me and Christy battered that cat without a lick o' help from you.

Joey   Being *associated* with cat battering, I'm saying.

Brendan   Well, don't claim credit for battering a cat you never lifted a finger to batter.

Joey   I won't claim credit for battering a cat, because there *is* no credit in battering a cat. Battering a cat is easy. There's no guts involved in cat battering. That sounds like something the fecking British'd do. Round up some poor Irish cats and give them a blast in the back as the poor devils were trying to get away, like on Bloody Sunday.

Brendan   They never shot cats on Bloody Sunday, did they, Christy?

Joey   It's the same principle I'm saying, ya thick.

Brendan   Oh, the same principle.

Joey   I'd've never joined the INLA in the first place if I'd known the battering of cats was to be on the agenda. The INLA has gone down in my estimation today. Same as when we blew up Airey Neave. You can't blow up a fella just because he has a funny name. It wasn't his fault.

Christy   Why don't you form a splinter group, so, like oul Mad Padraic?

Brendan   Aye. The Irish National Being Nice To Cats Army.

Joey   I would. Only I know you two'd blow me away for it, after probably killing me goldfish first!

Brendan   Sure, you've no goldfish, Joey.

Joey   I was making a fecking comparison!

Christy (*pause*)   We none of us enjoyed killing that cat, Joey-o. I was near crying meself, even as I brought me gun swinging down the fourth and fifth times, and the blood spraying out of him. But hasn't it worked? Haven't we lured the Madman of Aran home to where never once will he be looking behind him for that bolt from the blue he knows is some day coming? It won't be so quick then he'll be to go forming splinter groups, and knocking down fellas like poor Skank Toby, fellas who only do the community a service, and do they force anybody to buy their drugs? No. And don't they pay us a pound on every bag they push to go freeing Ireland for them? Isn't it for everybody we're out freeing Ireland? That's what Padraic doesn't understand, is it isn't only for the schoolkids and the oul fellas and the babes unborn we're out freeing Ireland. No. It's for the junkies, the thieves and the drug pushers too!

Joey   Aye. And for the cat batterers on top of it!

Brendan *and* **Christy** *stare hatefully at* **Joey** *a second, then slowly get up, spread out, take out their guns and point them at him.* **Joey**, *scared, stands and points his gun back at them.*

Christy   I was making a good speech there and you ruined it!

Brendan   He did, Christy. He ruined your speech on you. Let's pepper him.

Joey   Ah, let's not point our guns at each other. Sure, we're all friends here.

Christy   I thought we were friends, aye, but then you keep dragging dead cats into the equation.

Joey   I'm sorry, Christy. I have a fondness for cats is all. I'm sorry.

Christy   You want to get your priorities right, boy. Is it happy cats or is it an Ireland free we're after?

Joey   It's an Ireland free, Christy. Although I'd like a combination of the two.

Christy *cocks his gun.*

Joey   It's an Ireland free, Christy.

Pause. **Christy** *lowers his gun and collects his belongings. After a second the other two put their guns away also.*

Christy   Good. For won't the cats of Ireland be happier too when they won't have the English coming over bothering them no more?

Joey   They will.

Christy   Do you know how many cats Oliver Cromwell killed in his time?

Brendan   Lots of cats.

Christy   Lots of cats. And burned them alive. We have a way to go before we're in that bastard's league. We'll have not another word on the cat matter. Collect up your gear.

We'll lie low in a barn or somewhere tonight. Twelve noon the little fat lad said Padraic wouldn't be home till, and he had no need to lie. We'll arrive at ten past, and enter blasting.

The others collect their gear and move off left.

Christy   Did I tell you how I fecked up the fat fecker with his sister, saying it was him killed the cat? I said, 'The Jesuits say you should never tell a lie, boy, so I'll have to tell the truth on that subject.' Ha ha.

Brendan   Except it isn't the Jesuits who say that at all.

Christy   Is it not? Who is it then?

Brendan   I don't know, but it isn't the Jesuits.

Christy   Are you starting again?

Brendan   Starting what?

Christy   Starting your saying who didn't say things.

Brendan   I'm not starting anything. I'm just saying it isn't the Jesuits.

Christy   So who is it?

Brendan   I don't know!

Christy   I suppose it was fecking Marx!

Brendan (*exiting*)   It may have been fecking Marx. I do not know. What I'm saying for sure is it isn't the fecking Jesuits.

Christy (*exiting*)   Get ahead on the fecking road, you!

The voices of the three fade to mumbles off stage. Pause. **Mairead** *idles on from stage right, having overheard their conversation. She stares off after the men a second, broods thoughtfully, then cocks her air rifle. Blackout.*

Scene Six

Another roadside. Night, moonlight. **Mairead**, *in lipstick and a little make-up for once, leans against a wall, singing quietly 'The Patriot Game', the air rifle on the wall beside her.*

Mairead (*singing*)   'Come all ye young rebels and list while I sing. The love of one's land is a terrible thing. It banishes fear with the speed of a flame, and it makes us all part of the patriot game.'

Padraic *enters right and slowly moves along the road towards her. Though she's noticed him she continues singing.*

Mairead (*singing*)   'Oh my name is O'Hanlon, and I've just gone sixteen. My home is in Monaghan, there I was weaned. I was taught all my life cruel England's to blame, and so I'm a part of the patriot game.'

Padraic *stops in front of her, having joined in on her last line. They look at each other a while.*

Padraic   It's a while since I heard that oul song. Wasn't it one of the Behans wrote that?

Mairead   It was. Dominic.

Padraic (*about to move on*)   If they'd done a little more bombing and a little less writing I'd've had more respect for them.

Mairead   I still have respect for them. Lieutenant.

Padraic (*pause*)   You're not Seamus Claven's daughter?

Mairead   I am. You remembered me, so.

Padraic   I remember you chasing me begging to bring you when I left to free the North, and that when you were ten.

Mairead   Eleven. I'm sixteen now. If you get me meaning. Haven't I grown up since?

Padraic   You have. Upwards if not outwards. From a distance I thought 'What's a boy doing sitting there with lipstick on?', then as I got closer I realised it was a lass, just with shocking hair.

Mairead (*hiding hurt*)   Is that a nice thing to say to a girl comes to meet you off the boat the early morning?

Padraic   I suppose it's not, but that's the way I am.

Mairead   The girls must be falling over themselves to get to you in Ulster so, if them's the kind of compliments you be paying them.

Padraic   A few have fallen but I paid no mind. Not while there was work to be done ridding Erin of them jackboot hirelings of England's foul monarchy, and a lot of the girls up North are dogs anyways, so it was no loss.

Mairead   Do you prefer Inishmore girls, so?

Padraic   I don't.

Mairead   You don't prefer boys?

Padraic   I do not prefer boys! There's no boy-preferers involved in Irish terrorism, I'll tell you that! They stipulate when you join.

Mairead   Good, cos there's a dance at the church hall Friday would you take me to?

Padraic   Amn't I after telling you? I'm interested in no social activities that don't involve the freeing of Ulster.

Mairead   But that narrows it down terrible.

Padraic   So be it.

Mairead (*pause*)   There's a film on at the Omniplex about the Guildford Four next week. Isn't that close enough?

Padraic   Ah, feck the Guildford Four. Even if they didn't do it, they should've took the blame and been proud. But no, they did nothing but whine.

Mairead   We could go Dutch!

Padraic (*gently*)   No, Mairead. (*Pause.*) Why *did* you come to meet me this far out of your way?

Mairead (*sulkily*)   No reason.

Padraic   Just to ask me out, was it? Ah. (*Ruffles her hair.*) I see you still have your oul popgun there you wanted to give me that day. A lot of use that would've been to me up North.

Mairead   It does do the job for me OK.

Padraic   I suppose it does. There's not a heifer left with eyesight on Aran, I'll bet.

Mairead (*pacing angrily*)   Everybody slings me cow blinding at me, no matter how many years go by! What nobody ever mentions is it was from sixty yards I hit them cows' eyes, which is bloody good shooting in anybody's books. If I'd walked bang up to them I could understand it, but I didn't, I gave them every chance.

Padraic   Ah, hold your horses, Mairead, I was only fooling with you. I meself once shot a fella in the eye with a crossbow, but that was from right next to him. Sixty yards is marvellous going.

Mairead   You can't be getting round me that easy . . .

Padraic   Mairead, now . . .

Mairead   And you can forget the message I had for you too!

Padraic   What message?

Mairead   No message.

Padraic   No, what message did you have for me? (*Suddenly upset, suspicious.*) It wasn't me cat the message was about?

Mairead   If it was or if it wasn't I don't know, I have forgot.

Padraic *angrily pulls out both his guns and points them at* **Mairead**'s *head.*

Padraic   Tell me the fecking message now, ya bitcheen! Has me cat gone downhill or what the feck is it? Eh?

Poised, disgusted and superior, **Mairead** *picks up her air rifle, cocks it, and, while* **Padraic** *still has his guns to her head, points the rifle towards one of his eyes, so that the barrel is almost resting against it. Pause.*

Padraic   Do you think I'm joking?

Mairead   Do you think I am?

Padraic *(long pause)*   You have some balls, anyways.

Mairead   I don't have.

Padraic   I'll take your word.

Padraic *lowers his guns.* **Mairead** *pauses a moment or two, her rifle still up to his face, then she lowers it also.*

Mairead   Will you let me join up this time when you go back, so, if I'm such a tough oul feck with balls?

Padraic   We don't be letting girls in the INLA. No. Unless pretty girls. What was the message?

Mairead *(almost tearful)*   Unless pretty girls? Not even middling-looking girls who can put a cow's eye out from sixty yards?

Padraic   No. We have no call for girls with them attributes.

Mairead   Unfair to women that sounds.

Padraic   No, just fair to cows. *(Pause.)* What was the message, Mairead? Was it about my Wee Thomas, now?

Mairead   Your final word on the matter is you won't let me in the INLA, so? Not ever?

Padraic   Not as long as I have any say in the INLA. It's for your own good I'm saying this, Mairead. Be staying home, now, and marry some nice fella. Let your hair grow out a tadeen and some fella's bound to be looking twice at you some day, and if you learn how to cook and sew too, sure, that'd double your chances. Maybe treble.

Mairead (*pause*)   The message was Wee Thomas is over the worst of it, but be hurrying home to him, just to be on the safe side, now.

Padraic   He's over the worst of it?

Mairead   He is.

Padraic (*ecstatic*)   Oh, God love you, Mairead, I could kiss you!

Padraic *grabs* **Mairead** *in his arms and kisses her, a kiss of thanks at first, which lengthens into something much more sensual. They break, both a little disturbed.* **Padraic** *smiles uncomfortably and hurries off stage left.* **Mairead** *stares at the ground a while, singing quietly to herself, but with a little more thought for the words than before.*

Mairead (*singing*)   'And now as I lie with my body all holed . . . I think of the traitors who bargained and sold . . . And I'm sorry my rifle has not done the same . . . for the Quislings who sold out the patriot game.'

Mairead *looks off stage left after* **Padraic**. *Blackout.*

Scene Seven

Early blue dawn. **Donny**'s *house. Five o'clock.* **Donny** *and* **Davey** *still boozed,* **Donny** *in the armchair left, sleepy,* **Davey** *sitting on the floor right, holding a wooden cross he's made, its lower piece sharpened to a point, and along the crosspiece of which he finger-paints in shoe polish the words 'Wee Thomas'. The shoe-polished cat from earlier idles around where he pleases. Empty cat basket on table left.*

Donny   Remember now.

Davey   I'll remember. (*Pause.*) Remember what?

Donny   To be waking me!

Davey   Aye.

Donny   There's nothing more can be done till we're sober and it's light out, so we'll have a wee sleep and be up bright and early to fix the final touches so not a thing will he suspect.

Davey   Aye.

Donny   So be remembering to be waking me.

Davey (*yawning*)   I will.

Donny   You're a light sleeper, so you say.

Davey   I'm an awful light sleeper. Not only that, I have a thing in me head I can force meself to wake up bang on any hour I've decided on the night before. And not only the hour. The minute! Y'know, like a ninja.

Donny   How did you get that in your head?

Davey   It's a thing I've had since I was a child.

Donny   Creepy, that sounds.

Davey   Aye, it is creepy.

Donny   Set your head for nine in the morning, so.

Davey   Me head is set, you do not have to ask.

Donny (*pause*)   What's that you're doing?

Davey *shows* **Donny** *the finished cross.*

Davey   It's a cross for Wee Thomas. Look, it says 'Wee Thomas'.

Donny   That's a well-made cross.

Davey   *I* think it is, but it has to be drying, now.

Davey *sets the cross face down on the floor, taps it for luck, puts the cat in the cat basket, giving him a pat, and goes and sits in the armchair right, huddling up in it for sleep.*

Donny   In the morning, too, we'll have to go over the place with a toothcomb to make sure we've left nothing to give the game away his cat's dead.

Davey   We will, aye, although I think we've covered everything.

Donny (*pause*)   And you'll be remembering to wake me?

Davey   Me head is set for nine, Donny. I'm going to get angry soon.

Donny   Nighty-night, so.

Davey   Nighty-night, aye.

Donny   Don't let the bedbugs be biting.

Davey   I won't let them.

The two men sit there, falling asleep. Slow fade to black.

Donny   And you'll remember to be waking me?

Davey *looks across at* **Donny** *sternly.* **Donny** *sniggers.* **Davey** *laughs too. They settle down to sleep.*

Scene Eight

Donny's *house. Twelve noon.* **Donny** *and* **Davey** *asleep in their armchairs, hands still black. Thomas's cross still lying on the floor, the polished cat asleep in the cat basket, only half visible, purring.*
Padraic *enters through the front door quietly, happily and, on seeing the two men asleep, calls out in a whisper, looking for his cat.*

Padraic   Thomas? Wee Thomas? Here, baby. Daddy's home. Are you not well, loveen? I've some ringworm pellets here for ya.

Pause. **Padraic** *notices the cat asleep in the basket, goes over to it and, confused, runs his fingers along its back. His fingers come away black and he smells them. He idles back to the sleeping* **Davey**, *spots* **Davey**'s *black hands, raises one of them to get a better look at it, then lets it drop.* **Davey** *remains asleep. Still confused,* **Padraic** *notices the cross on the floor and picks it up. As he reads its inscription his face drops, from sadness to fury, just as* **Davey** *begins to wake, stretch his arms, open his eyes and see* **Padraic**.

Davey   Feck me!

Padraic *storms over to* **Davey**, *wrenches him up by the hair, takes a gun out and points it at* **Davey**'s *head.* **Davey** *whimpers, waking* **Donny**.

Padraic (*to* **Davey**)   Where's me cat? Eh? Where's me fecking cat?

Donny (*sleepily*)   Are you home, Padraic?

Davey   I forgot to wake you, Donny!

Padraic   Where's me fecking cat, I said?

Still whimpering, **Davey** *points a shaky finger at the cat basket.* **Donny**, *regaining his senses, is now fearful too.*

Padraic   Eh?

Donny   He has a disease makes him go orangey, Padraic.

Padraic   Oh, he has a disease makes him go orangey, does he?

Davey (*high-pitched, breathless*)   And smell of shoe polish!

Padraic *drags* **Davey** *to the cat basket.* **Donny** *stands.*

Padraic   So this is Wee Thomas, is it?

Donny   It is.

Davey   It is.

Donny   We think.

Padraic   Oh, hello there, Wee Thomas. It's nice to be seeing you again after all this time.

Donny   I suppose he's changed since last you saw him, Padraic. Oh, cats do change quick.

Padraic   Changed quick, is it, Dad?

He shoots the sleeping cat, point blank. It explodes in a ball of blood and bones. **Davey** *begins screaming hysterically.* **Donny** *puts his hands to his head.* **Padraic** *shoves* **Davey***'s face into the bloody cat to stop him screaming.*

He's changed quick enough now! And ye two'll be changing the same way in a minute. Where's Wee Thomas? For the fiftieth fecking time, this is!

Donny   We think he's run away!

Padraic   You think he's run away, do ye?

He takes **Davey***'s head out of the cat, forces him to his knees, lunges over to* **Donny***, grabs him by the hair and kneels him down beside* **Davey***.*

Is that why these shenanigans?

Padraic *angrily holds up the dead bloody cat from the basket, then throws it in through the door to the bathroom stage left.*

Is that why this fecking thing, so?

Padraic *bangs* **Donny** *in the face with the crucifix and holds it in front of him.*

Donny (*to* **Davey**)   I knew you'd made a mistake somewhere along the line, you!

Padraic   Is Wee Thomas dead, now? Answer me!

Donny (*pause*)   He is, Padraic.

Padraic *puts his head in his hands and lets out a long, deep moan, backing off around the room.*

Davey   We did see him in the road, Padraic . . .

Donny   We didn't see him in the road at all, Padraic. This fella clobbered him with his bike and then pegged stones at him.

Davey   Not at all, Padraic!

Donny   Admitted, he has!

Davey   Ahead in the lonely road I saw him lying, and ran him inside then as quick as me legs could carry me, and me only crime, if I have one at all, was moving the victim before professional help arrived, but with Wee Tommy's head strung a mile o'er the road, I assumed the niceties wouldn't be necessry.

Donny   And pegged stones, Padraic.

Davey   Pegged stones me arse! This from a fella feeds his cat nothing but Frosties.

Donny   I do not feed him Frosties, Padraic! I buy cat food and *good* cat food. Sheba half the time, I buy.

Davey   Sheba bollocks, and I'll give you a pound if any Sheba you can find in this feck's cupboards . . .

Padraic (*screaming*)   Shut up!!

Donny   I *do* buy Sheba, Padraic . . .

Padraic *rifles through a couple of drawers until he finds some rope, which he then uses to tie* **Donny**'s *hands to his feet behind his back.*

Donny (*scared*)   Oh, Padraic, don't be tying me hands behind me back, now. We know what you be doing to fellas their hands you tie behind their back . . .

Davey   What does he be doing to them, Donny? Tickling them.

Donny *gives him a look.*

Davey (*crying*)   I was just trying to keep me hopes up.

Padraic *ties* **Davey** *in the same way as* **Donny**, *during which* **Davey** *manages to get up some nerve.*

Davey (*angrily*)   Sure, I was only trying to save the feck was how I became involved!

Padraic   So me cat is a feck now, is he?

Davey   He is! And you are too, Padraic Osbourne! And I don't care if you do blow the head off me. You're a mad thick feck and everybody knows that you are! So there!

Donny (*shocked*)   Oh, Davey boy . . .

Padraic   Let's see you with a bit of a haircut, so, if I'm such a mad thick feck.

Padraic *takes out a bowie knife and starts roughly hacking off all of* **Davey**'s *hair.*

Davey   Ar, not me hair! Sure, this just confirms you're a mad thick feck!

Padraic   I'd be scared the bullets wouldn't be getting through this girl's minge.

Donny   Ah, don't be killing us, Padraic. Sure, we didn't mean for Wee Thomas to die.

Padraic   Wee Thomas was in your care. Me only friend in the world for fifteen years, and then into your care I put him . . .

Davey   Fifteen years? Sure, he'd had a good innings, Padraic. Aargh!

Padraic   And Wee Thomas is now dead. Them's the only facts this tribunal needs.

Donny   What tribunal?

Davey   Them facts are only circumstantial.

The haircut finished, **Padraic** *tosses the knife aside and takes out his two handguns.*

Padraic   These guns are only circumstantial, so, and so too your brains'll be only circumstantial as they leave your heads and go skidding up the wall.

Davey   That sentence makes no sense at all.

Donny (*to* **Davey**)   Do you have to get him even more worked up, you?

Padraic *puts a gun to the back of each of their heads.*

Padraic   Be making any final confession you have, now, before you go meeting yere maker. Maybe a rabbit you knifed, or a pony you throttled.

Davey   I'm making no confession because there's nothing in the world I've done wrong.

Padraic (*to* **Donny**)   What about you?

Donny (*pause*)   I confess, so, to feeding him Frosties now and then, but only now and then, Padraic, and there does be nutrition in Frosties, and the fella seemed to like them.

Padraic   And that's all you confess? Well, straight to hell you'll be going, so, because I know well a hundred other crimes you've committed in your time.

Donny   What other crimes?

Padraic   We don't have time to be making out a full list, but trampling on your mam all them times'll do for a start-off.

Davey   You *did* trample on your mam!

Donny   Ten years ago, that was!

Padraic   There's no statute of limitations on mam trampling, Dad. Now shut up while I make me speech.

Still pointing the guns at their heads, **Padraic** *cocks them.* **Donny** *and* **Davey** *shiver tearfully. The clock on the wall is just reaching twelve ten.*

Padraic   Ye have killed me cat and ye've ruined me life, for what I've got to live for now I do not know . . .

Davey   You could get another cat.

Padraic *hits* **Davey** *with the butt of his gun.*

Padraic   I will plod on, I know, but no sense to it will
there be with Thomas gone. No longer will his smiling eyes
be there in the back of me head, egging me on, saying, 'This
is for me and for Ireland, Padraic. Remember that,' as I'd
lob a bomb at a pub, or be shooting a builder. Me whole
world's gone, and he'll never be coming back to me. (*Pause.*)
What I want ye to remember, as the bullets come out
through yere foreheads, is that this is all a fella can be
expecting for being so bad to an innocent Irish cat.
Goodbye to ye, now.

Donny *and* **Davey** *tense up.*

Padraic   *Goodbye*, I said.

Davey   Goodbye . . .

Donny   Goodbye, Padraic . . .

Donny *and* **Davey** *tense up again. Pause. There is a loud knock at
the front door.* **Padraic** *uncocks his guns.*

Padraic (*sighing*)   You could've told me you were
expecting someone.

Donny   I wasn't.

Padraic *goes to the door.*

Padraic   Well, don't try anything or ye'll be getting it
worse.

Davey (*whispered to* **Donny**)   Sure, how can we get it any
worse, sure?

Padraic *opens the front door wide. Standing there are* **Christy**,
Joey *and* **Brendan**, *smiling, their hands behind their backs.*
Padraic *laughs, happy to see them.*

Christy   Howdo.

Padraic   Christy! What the feck are you fellas doing out this way? Come on in ahead for yourselves. I'm just in the middle of shooting me dad.

*He turns his back on them, goes back to the two kneeling men and points his guns at their heads, at the same time as the three men at the door dash in, take the guns out from behind their backs and point them right up against **Padraic***'s head – one on the left side, one on the right and one from behind, in something of a triangle.*

Padraic (*pause*)   What's all this about, now?

Christy   Does the word 'splinter group' mean anything to ya?

Padraic   'Splinter group'? 'Splinter group's two words.

Christy   Mister Cocksure, uh-huh.

Brendan   Hah. He's not so cocksure now, is he, Christy?

Christy   He's not.

Joey   He *is*.

Christy   Shush, now, Joey . . .

Joey   Well, he *is*. He's still cocksure. Look at him . . .

Christy   All *right*, Joey. For feck's *sake*, now. (*Pause.*) Throw your guns on the table there, Padraic, and easy.

Padraic *pauses a moment, then does so.*

Christy   Skank Toby was the last straw, Padraic. Messing around teasing your marijuana gobshites is fine. But when you drag one of the big-time boys into the equation, a fella without whom there'd be no financing for your ferry crossings and your chip-shop manoeuvres, and not only to cut the nose off him, all well and good, a bit of micro-surgery may do the trick later, but to then feed it to his cocker spaniel, a dog never did no one harm, and choked himself to death on it . . .

Padraic   I don't like dogs, I don't.

Donny   He was frightened be a corgi as a little fella.

Christy   And made Skank Toby watch that dog choke, and sticking your finger in where his nose was then if he tried to help it, and when then you talk of splinter groups, and splinter groups of two fellas, which isn't a splinter group at all, it's just two fellas.

Brendan   In a mood.

Christy   In a mood. No, boy. That's the time we've got to take a long hard look at ourselves and say 'All this has got to end, now. Uh-huh. All this has got to end.'

Padraic   You've always had it in for me, Christy. And for no reason at all.

Christy   No reason, no. Other than you shooting me fecking eye out, ya bastard.

Padraic   I've apologised for that eye many's the day.

Christy   Playing 'murder in the dark' with a crossbow, like a schoolchild.

Padraic   You never let bygones be bygones, you.

Christy *cocks his gun.* **Joey** *and* **Brendan** *do likewise.*

Padraic   Christy, now? You wouldn't be killing a fella in front of his dad, would ya?

Brendan   You're behind your dad.

Padraic   It's the *principle* I'm saying, ya thick, Brendan.

Brendan   Oh, the principle.

Padraic   Dad, you wouldn't want to see me killed in front of you, would ya? Wouldn't it be a trauma?

Donny   I couldn't give a feck! Weren't you about to shoot me in the fecking head, sure?

Padraic   Ah, I was only tinkering with ya, Dad. Do you think I'd've done it?

Donny Aye!

Davey Aye!

Padraic Take me out on the road, Christy. No one ever comes down that lonely road. Not a struggle I'll give to ya. I knew this'd be coming some day. I just didn't think so soon, and from friends. Just walk me to a ditch. The burying will be all the easier for you. Only it'll give me a minute to be saying a prayer for me poor cat, died recently, the self-same road.

Brendan (*smiling*) Your poor cat, is it?

Padraic It is. Why?

Christy (*raising a cautionary finger*) Erm . . .

Brendan (*thinking quickly*) Erm . . . We heard tell of your cat dying . . . and sad we were you were to have the two spots of bad news in the one week, your cat dying and your being shot through the brains yourself. That's awful hard luck.

Padraic And I'll tell you this, boys. One of them spots of news does make me sadder than the other, but I'll bet in a hundred years you couldn't guess which.

Joey Your cat dying makes you sadder.

Padraic Is right, Joey. You was always the sensitive one.

Joey Thank you, Padraic, I always tried.

Christy Tie his hands, Joe. We'll walk him the road for himself. For there's no terrible hard feelings in this execution. You was always a good soldier, Padraic. Just overenthusiastic.

Joey *ties* **Padraic**'s *hands behind his back.* **Padraic** *looks around the room.*

Padraic Full of memories of Wee Thomas this house is. How asleep in me arms he'd fall, the armchair there. Aye, and purr and yawn. How he'd pooh in a corner when you were drunk and you'd forget to let him out, and he'd look embarrassed the next day then, as if it was his fault, the poor lamb. How in through the hole in the wall there he'd come, after a two-day bender chasing skirt the length of the island, and pulling your hair out for fear something had happened to him you'd be, and him prancing in then like 'What was all the fuss about? I was off getting me end away.' (*Pause.*) He won't be prancing in today.

Davey (*half laughing*)   Indeed he won't be.

Padraic   What d'you mean 'Indeed he won't be'?

Davey   No, I'm just saying it does be awful hard to prance when you're buried in shite, your head knocked out your arse.

His hands tied, **Padraic** *tries to lunge out at* **Davey** *with his feet. The three gunmen restrain him and start dragging him to the door.*

Come on indeed, ya oul mad hole, ya!

Padraic   I'll fecking kill ya!

Davey   Kill me so, aye, and cut the rest of me hair off while you're at it, ya bully!

Christy   Get him outside . . .

Padraic   Ya fecking cat killer, ya . . .

Davey   Eight years it took me to grow that hair!

Padraic   I'll be back to get ya! (*To* **Donny**.) And you too!

Davey   In your dreams you'll be back, ya lube.

Padraic   Not in me dreams at all. In ten minutes.

Christy   You won't be back in ten minutes, Padraic. You'll be dead in ten minutes.

Padraic   We'll be seeing about that! I'd've gone easy till this feck chipped in!

Christy   We have three guns to your head and you're bound be rope, sure.

Padraic   Something'll turn up!

Joey   What does he mean, Christy? 'Something'll turn up'?

Christy (*exiting*)   He's just trying to make you nervous, Joey.

Joey (*exiting*)   He's fecking succeeded, Christy.

Brendan (*exiting*)   Didn't I tell you he'd shit himself, Christy?

Padraic (*exiting*)   I'll be back again for you, long-hair boy!

Davey   Do! And bring your drippy cat with you! Ye can both take me on! Ye'd still lose!

Padraic (*distantly*)   Something'll turn up! I can feel it!

Long silent pause. The gunmen and **Padraic** *have gone.* **Donny** *and* **Davey** *are still tied, kneeling.*

Davey   Has he always been that way, Donny?

Donny   I think he may have gotten worse, now.

Davey (*pause*)   Are you sad, Donny?

Davey   Sad, why?

Davey   Sad them fellas are to be shooting your son's head off him?

Donny (*pause*)   Not really, if I think about it, now.

Davey   No. After your son tries to execute you, your opinions do change about him.

Donny   You lose respect, d'you know?

Davey (*pause*)   They could've untied us. It wouldn't have killed them. (*Pause.*) Actually it *might've* killed them, come to think of it.

Donny It might've, aye. They had to concentrate at all times with that mad feck.

Davey Let them concentrate a minute more and that'll be the end of it. Your son will be dead and them fecks will be gone, and Inishmore can get back to normal then.

Donny Is right. It's incidents like this does put tourists off Ireland.

Davey Aye. (*Pause.*) 'He'll be back again for me.' He isn't back yet, nor will he be back.

Donny (*pause*) Did you hear a noise?

Davey What kind of a noise?

Donny A clicking?

Davey No.

Donny Oh.

Davey Did you?

Donny No.

Davey Oh.

Donny Good.

Davey Aye.

*Pause, then the unmistakable sound of the rapid fire, from somewhere outside, of **Mairead**'s air rifle . . .*

Davey Ar, not me fecking sister, now!

*. . . followed immediately by the hideous screaming of the three gunmen. Sound of gunfire being returned, as the screams continue, getting louder and louder as the screamers get nearer to the house, till suddenly **Brendan** smashes in through the window left and **Joey** and **Christy** burst in through the door. All three are bleeding profusely from their eyes, at which they clutch and tear, blinded, still screaming, crawling around the floor. **Donny** and **Davey** watch them in horror.*

Brendan I can't fecking see! I can't fecking see!

Joey   She's had our fecking eyes out!

Christy   Are ye blinded too?

Brendan   We fecking are!

Christy   Was it a boy or was it a girl?

Brendan   It was a boy with lipstick.

Joey   It was a girl with no boobs, sure.

Brendan   Oh, don't let me be killed by a girl, Sweet Jesus!
I'll never live it down.

Joey   Mam and Dad'll be terrible sad, eh, Brendan, the
two of us killed the same day?

Brendan   Oh, they'll be choked, Joey. I *do* love you,
y'know, Joe. I'm sorry if I never showed it ya.

Joey   I love you too, Brendan!

Christy   Ar, stop that shite! Get firing, now!

All three gunmen begin shooting madly, **Brendan** *through the left
window,* **Christy** *through the right and* **Joey** *through the doorway.*

Christy   Are you two tied fellas still here?

Davey   Aye.

Donny   Aye. No!!

Davey   No!!

Donny *quietly shoulder-knudges* **Davey** *in irritation for giving
away their presence.*

Christy   Well call out the right direction for us to be
shooting, so, or ye'll be getting it too.

Just then, **Padraic** *and* **Mairead** *appear in the doorway, hand in
hand, quietly stepping around* **Joey**'*s line of fire as they enter,*
Mairead *carrying her air rifle,* **Padraic** *pulling the last of the
ropes off his hands.*

Donny (*to* **Christy**)   Erm, left a biteen . . .

The three gunmen, still firing out of the windows and door, aim towards the left. **Padraic** *and* **Mairead** *seem to almost glide across the room, their eyes locked on each other.* **Padraic** *caresses her hair and cheek, impressed beyond words at her abilities with a gun.*

Donny   Erm, right a bit, now . . .

Brendan   They must be zigzagging! Are they?

Donny   They are.

Brendan   The fecks!

The gunmen shoot towards the right. **Padraic** *and* **Mairead** *step over to where the two handguns lie on the table and* **Padraic** *picks them up. They move up behind* **Brendan** *and, with* **Mairead** *caressing the muscles in his back and shoulders,* **Padraic** *puts both guns up to* **Brendan**'s *head and fires, killing him instantly. With all the gunfire going on, the other two gunmen do not notice.* **Padraic** *and* **Mairead** *move slowly towards* **Joey**, *their eyes still locked in love.*

Christy   Are they getting nearer or are they getting away?

Padraic *shoots* **Joey** *in the head, again with the double-gun method at close quarters.* **Mairead** *gently toes* **Joey**'s *dead body.*

Donny   They're getting nearer.

Christy   How near?

Donny   Awful near.

Christy *runs out of bullets. As he tries to reload he realises all the other gunfire has stopped too.*

Christy   Fellas? Why've you stopped shooting, fellas? Fellas?

Pause. **Christy**'s *face drops as he realises* **Padraic** *is in the room. He tosses his gun away, sick.*

Not in me head, Padraic, please. For me mother's sake, now . . .

Padraic *double-shoots* **Christy** *in the chest.* **Christy** *slumps back on to the floor, dying, but not actually dead.* **Padraic** *and*

Mairead *move up to each other and kiss, as* **Donny** *and* **Davey** *look on, still kneeling there, bound and trembling.*

Donny   That was some gutsy shooting, Padraic!

Davey   What's he kissing me fecking sister for?

Padraic *and* **Mairead** *slowly turn and look at the two.* **Padraic** *cocks his guns. The two tremble.*

Padraic   This fella's your brother, is he?

Mairead   He has a better hairstyle since last I saw him, but aye, he is.

Padraic   Oh. I was all set to blow his head off now, along with the feck beside him, but if he's family I won't. I'll have some respect. I'll kill me dad on his own.

Mairead *gently takes one of the guns from* **Padraic***, sidles up behind her brother and puts the gun to his head, speaking as she goes.*

Mairead   If I'm to be travelling back up North with you, I suppose I'll have to be getting used to proper guns some time.

Padraic   And there's no time like the present.

Mairead   None at all.

They smile at each other. **Padraic** *puts his gun to his dad's head,* **Mairead** *to* **Davey**'s.

Donny   No, now . . .

Davey   Ar, come on, now . . .

Donny   You're only tinkering with us again, aren't ye?

Padraic   On a count of three?

Mairead   On a count of three, aye. Like in films.

Davey   Ar, Jesus, Mairead, Jesus . . . !

Padraic   One . . . !

Donny   Goodbye now, Davey . . .

Davey   Goodbye now, Donny . . .

Padraic   Two . . . !

Donny   Unfair, this is!

Davey   Aren't they beggars?

Padraic   Three . . . !

Christy (*interrupting*)   I'm sorry for killing your cat, Padraic. I am, now.

Padraic (*pause*)   What was that, Christy?

Christy   I said I'm sorry for killing your cat on you. The worst part of all this was that cat braining, but you had to be knocked off your guard some way, and you'll admit how well it worked, now. Ar, boy. Just making me peace with God, I am, in the seconds before I slip away, now.

Padraic   Your peace, is it?

Christy   It is.

Padraic   Uh-huh. I'll give you some fecking peace, boy . . .

Padraic and **Mairead** *take their guns away from the kneelers' heads,* **Padraic** *chucks his on the table, goes over to* **Christy** *and starts dragging him by the neck into the adjoining room forward right, perhaps so that he's half out of sight.*

Padraic (*to* **Mairead**)   Bring a knife, a cheese grate, a razor, an iron and anything to gag the screaming, Mairead.

Mairead   Check, Lieutenant.

Mairead *puts her gun on the table and darts about, grabbing the objects just listed.* **Christy** *begins screaming hideously as* **Padraic** *tortures him, blood splattering.*

Donny   It's an ill wind that doesn't blow some fecker good!

Davey   Isn't it, though?

Blackout.

Scene Nine

Donny's *house, night. As the scene begins the blood-soaked living room is strewn with the body parts of* **Brendan** *and* **Joey**, *which* **Donny** *and* **Davey**, *blood-soaked also, hack away at to sizeable chunks.* **Padraic**'s *two guns are lying on the table. In the adjacent bare room,* **Padraic** *is sitting on* **Christy**'s *corpse, stroking Wee Thomas's headless, dirt-soiled body. Through* **Christy**'s *mouth, with the pointed end sticking out of the back of his neck, has been shoved the cross with 'Wee Thomas' on it.* **Padraic** *has a sad, faraway look about him. He cannot hear the quiet conversation* **Donny** *and* **Davey** *are having.*

Donny   Won't your mam be upset, your Mairead joining the paramilitaries, Davey?

Davey   She knew it was to be coming some day. I think she'll have resigned herself to it, though I think she'd have preferred it to be the IRA if anybody. Y'know, they're more established.

Donny   They are. And they do travel further afield than the INLA.

Davey   The IRA do get a good bit of travelling done, aye.

Donny   They do. They go to Belgium sometimes.

Davey   You never see the INLA going to Belgium.

Donny   You're lucky if they leave the Falls.

Davey   You never see the INLA shooting Australians.

Donny   Still, I suppose it isn't the travel that attracts people to the IRA.

Davey   No. It's the principle of the thing. I'll tell ya, I'd shit meself having to shoot fellas, but Mairead seems to have no qualms.

Donny   I'll say this about Mairead. She's fecking accurate. Knock your eye out from a mile.

Davey   I always knew that cow practising would pay off some day.

Donny   Padraic has an entirely different style.

Davey   Padraic goes all the way up to ya.

Donny   Padraic goes all the way up to ya, and then uses two guns from only an inch away.

Davey   Sure, there's no skill in that.

Donny   I think the two guns is overdoing it. From that range, like.

Davey   It's just showing off, really.

Donny   Mairead sees more of the sport. (*Pause.*) Is he still sitting on the fella and stroking the dead cat?

Davey (*craning his neck*)   He is. Morbid, that was, digging up his dead cat. After all the trouble we went to burying it, and without a word of thanks.

Donny   I suppose it does help the mourning process.

Davey (*pause*)   Digging up the corpse?

Donny shrugs. **Mairead** *has entered through the front door, wearing a pretty dress and carrying a rucksack and air rifle.*

Mairead   Less gabbing and more chopping would be more in ye's two's line.

Donny   I don't see you or your boyfriend giving us a hand . . .

Davey   What the hell's that you're wearing?

Mairead   A dress! I *do* have them!

Davey   Hrmm . . .

Mairead   Why should we be giving ye a hand?

Donny   It's yere mess, sure.

Mairead Well, it's your house. And you don't be getting officers doing this sort of dirty work, anyways.

Davey Oh, you're an officer now, are ya?

Mairead I'm a second-lieutenant. Just awarded be Padraic. Padraic's just awarded himself a full-blown lieutenantship, and he deserves it.

Donny Ye're all going up in the world.

Mairead Be knocking them teeth out them mouths, now. It does hamper the identification process.

Donny She's awful on the ball.

Mairead I am.

Davey What did Mam say to you when you left?

Mairead She said good luck and try not to go blowing up kids.

Davey And what did you say?

Mairead I said I'd try but I'd be making no promises.

Davey And what did she say?

Mairead She said so long as you try is the main thing.

Davey I suppose it is.

Mairead Oh, it is, but I can't be bandying about pleasantries with the likes of ye. Be getting on with your work, now. Them corpses won't be chopping themselves up, or d'ye think they will?

Mairead *passes through to* **Padraic**.

Davey She loves pegging orders, that one.

Donny I can see.

Donny *and* **Davey** *continue with their hacking and bludgeoning.* **Mairead** *sits down beside* **Padraic** *on* **Christy**'s *bloody corpse.*

Mairead Howdo.

Padraic   Howdo. (*Pause.*) There's no head at all on Wee Thomas now.

Mairead   No. Does it make you think twice about the INLA, so, that they let fellas like Christy in, would do that to a cat?

Padraic   Sure, you do get bad apples in every organisation. (*Pause.*) Are them wet fellas still chopping?

Mairead   Aye.

Padraic   Are they making a decent job of it?

Mairead   Middling.

Padraic   They've had no practice, sure, God bless them. (*Pause.*) What the hell's that you're wearing?

Mairead   Isn't a girl allowed to wear dresses now and again?

Padraic   Just that it comes as a shock is all.

Mairead   Would you say I looked pretty in it, or just fair, now?

Padraic *kisses her at length, the cat awkward in one hand. They break after a few seconds.*

Padraic   When you get up close to you, you don't really look like a boy at all.

Mairead   Thank you.

Padraic   Just except for your hair.

Mairead   From you that's some kind of compliment, I suppose?

Padraic   Would you let your hair be growing out a tadeen, Mairead? Just to about here, now. Like Evie off *The House of Elliot*?

Mairead   Would you like me to?

Padraic   Aye.

Mairead   Well, me hair's staying the way it is and feck Evie off *The House of Elliot.*

Padraic   Ah, Mairead . . .

Mairead   Could Evie blind three fellas from sixty yards?

Padraic   No. But she probably wouldn't want to.

Mairead   Just be content with what you've fecking got, so.

Padraic   You're a tough oul get.

Mairead   And fecking proud of it.

Padraic   Kiss me again.

Mairead   I will.

Padraic (*they kiss again. Pause*)   Will we leave the INLA altogether and be starting our own splinter group, just me and you?

Mairead   Would you like to?

Padraic   I would.

Mairead   We will so. What will we call ourselves?

Padraic   I was thinking 'Wee Thomas's Army', unless you have an objection, now.

Mairead   Sure, that sounds like a great name. 'Wee Thomas's Army'. Aye. What'll be our first plan of action?

Padraic   Our first plan of action will be to find a fella I owe a torturing to. I had him in me clutches yesterday, but the cat distractions made me go easy on the feck, I hardly touched him, and he spun me a yarn about ringworm proved completely untrue too. 'Wrapping pellets up in cheese'. I bet he doesn't even have a cat.

Mairead   He sounds like a valid target anyways.

Padraic   He's the validest of targets.

Mairead   We should make a list of valid targets. From one to twenty. Like *Top of the Pops*.

Padraic   I used to have a list of valid targets but I lost it on a bus. Who would be top of your list?

Mairead   People who brain cats for no reason.

Padraic   Is a good target. Although . . . (*Pause.*) Can I tell you this, Mairead? I did brain a cat this morning, but I did have a reason.

Mairead   What was the reason?

Padraic   It seemed terrible unhygienic. Half covered in black muck.

Mairead   Fair go, so. I don't like unhygienic cats. Braining nice clean cats, I'm saying. My cat I wanted to say goodbye to him, now I won't be seeing him for a while. Me best friend in the world he is, but he wasn't about. He must be off gallivanting.

Padraic   My cat won't be off gallivanting no more, and he liked a good gallivant.

Mairead   Ar, Padraic . . .

Padraic   Ah, Mairead. Y'know, all I ever wanted was an Ireland free. Free for kids to run and play. Free for fellas and lasses to dance and sing. Free for cats to roam about without being clanked in the brains with a handgun. Was that too much to ask, now? Was it?

Mairead   It seems it was, Padraic. It seems it was. Will we be bringing Wee Thomas with us or will we be burying him here?

Padraic   We'll bring him with us. I have a window box at home he can go in, so he'll be near his friends.

Mairead (*standing*)   Would you want to bring his crucifix, so?

Padraic (*standing*)   No. That crucifix is too big for my window box. It'd break me chrysanthemums.

Hand in hand, they enter the living room.

Padraic   How is the work going, ye's two?

Donny   We're almost there, Padraic. Almost there.

Padraic   You're not almost there at all, sure. The fingerprints you haven't burnt off and the teeth you haven't bludgeoned out. And One-eyed Christy you haven't even started on. 'Ye're almost there.' You won't be almost there for a week, sure.

Davey   Why we should be doing this work at all I don't see. It wasn't us murdered them. If it was us murdered them I'd say 'fair go', but no.

Padraic   Are you grumbling again, you?

Davey (*mumbling*)   I fecking am.

Padraic   Eh?

Davey   No, I'm not grumbling.

Padraic   I'd've been kicking your balls out your brains long since, you, ya feck, only it's sure I am you'll be being me brother-in-law some day, and that'd be a bad show that'd be, kicking your brother-in-law's balls out his brains.

Mairead *gazes up at* **Padraic** *lovingly.*

Mairead   Is it marriage you're proposing to me so, Padraic Osbourne?

Padraic   It is. After a biteen of a while I'm saying, now. When our work is done.

Mairead   When Ireland is free!

Padraic   Indeed when Ireland is free!

They kiss at length.

Donny   That'll be a long fecking engagement!

Davey　Fecking a hundred they'll be, and still waiting.

Donny　Won't that make you and me related so, when them two marry?

Davey (*with disdain*)　It fecking will too.

Donny　What matter?

Davey　Do you think I want to be related to mad gunmen and mam tramplers?

Donny　Do you think I want to be related to gay hippies and cat polishers?

Davey (*quietly, in awful realisation*)　Oh, feck, now! All about that fecking cat I forgot!

Davey *goes over to the bloody cat basket on the table stage left, checks inside for the cat but finds it empty, puts the basket aside, looks around a little more, shoving a head or an arm aside, then finds Sir Roger's collar and name tag on the cabinet stage left. He is just about to toss it out through the broken window when* **Padraic** *and* **Mairead** *separate.*

Padraic　Look at you in that pretty dress. Oh, God, now! Half-covered it in blood we have.

Mairead　Ah, what matter? Red goes well with it.

Padraic　You can't go walking the streets of Ulster dripping blood, now.

Mairead　Sure, who would notice, Padraic?

Padraic　Tourists would notice. Be changing it or washing it off, now.

Mairead　I'll give it a wee rinse for meself, so.

Davey *tosses the collar out through the window.*

Mairead　What are you up to?

Davey　Nothing at all.

Mairead　Be desecting them fecks, you.

Davey   I was just waving me arms.

Mairead   Uh-huh. And you say Padraic's mad?

She moves towards bathroom left.

Can you bear to be away from me five minutes, me love?

Padraic   I can't. Be hurrying.

Mairead   I will.

Mairead *blows him a kiss and exits into bathroom.*

Padraic (*calling out*)   Oh, and be minding that oul grubby cat on the floor there I did blow the guts out of.

Davey's *mouth drops slightly and he stares off towards the bathroom.*

Padraic (*to* **Davey**)   So you be saying I'm mad, do ya?

Davey (*absently*)   I do.

Padraic   Eh?

Davey   Eh?

Padraic   I'm saying you be saying I'm mad, do ya?

Davey (*absently*)   I do.

Padraic   Eh?!

Davey   Eh?

Davey *looks across at* **Padraic** *for the first time, unaware of any discourtesy.*

Padraic   You're a funny little fella. Be getting back to work, now. Do you think them corpses'll be chopping themselves up?

Donny   They won't be, Padraic. Davey, what's the matter with you? Come back down here and start hammering some teeth.

Davey (*absently*)   I'll be hammering, aye.

He kneels back down beside **Donny** *and starts absent-mindedly hammering the teeth out of one of the heads, his eyes on the bathroom all the while.*

Worse and worse and worse this story gets.

Donny   What are you saying, Davey?

Davey   Worse and fecking worse.

Padraic   That boy's near simple.

Donny   He's an odd little gasur. He seems to have no proper sense. (*Pause. Sawing.*) Boy, spines are awful hard sawing, I'll tell ya.

Padraic   Aren't they, though? Be aiming for the vertebree is easiest.

Donny   The vertebree, I was thinking.

Mairead *appears blank-eyed in the doorway of the bathroom, clutching the body of the bloody and black Sir Roger to her chest.* **Davey** *has seen her, the other two haven't.*

Donny   Have I congratulated you on your engagement yet, son?

Padraic   You haven't.

Donny (*getting up*)   Congratulations on your engagement, son.

Padraic   Thanks, Dad.

Donny *shakes* **Padraic**'s *hand.* **Mairead** *enters the room and* **Padraic** *notices her for the first time.*

Padraic   Look at you. We have a matching pair. One fecked cat each. Who says we have nothing in common but shooting fellas? No, I shouldn't be joking like that. Not about poor Wee Thomas, now.

Mairead   Not about Sir Roger neither, no.

Padraic   Sir Roger who? Sir Roger Casement?

Mairead   Aye.

Padraic   What has that oul poof got to do with dead cats, Mairead?

Mairead *gently hands her cat down to* **Davey***, smiles slightly at him and brushes a bloody hand through his short hair. She turns back to* **Padraic***, whose back is to the table, the two handguns behind him. He caresses her cheek gently, as she quietly begins singing 'The Dying Rebel'.*

Mairead (*singing*)   'The night was dark and the fight was ended . . .'

Padraic *joins in.*

Both   'The moon shone down O'Connell Street . . .'

Mairead   Kiss me, Padraic.

Padraic *kisses her at length and, as he does so,* **Mairead** *reaches down behind him, picks one gun up in each hand, slowly raises them and points them one on each side of* **Padraic***'s head.* **Padraic** *is unaware of this.* **Donny** *looks on in horror. The kiss is finished.*

Padraic   What's the next line now, Mairead? (*Singing.*) 'The moon shone down O'Connell Street . . .'

Mairead   There was nothing unhygienic about my fecking cat.

Padraic (*pause*)   No, it's something to do with brave men perishing, I think.

Mairead   Aye.

She shoots **Padraic** *in the head with both guns.* **Padraic** *falls back on the table behind him, dead, his cat still clutched in his arms, his mouth wide open.* **Mairead** *looks at the guns in her hands a while, as she quietly continues with the song.*

(*Singing.*) 'I stood alone where brave men perished. Those men have gone, their God to meet.'

She places the barrels of both guns in **Padraic**'s *mouth, leaves them there and gently takes her cat back off* **Davey**.

Be chopping up that feck too, now, the two of ye.

Donny   Sure, you can't be asking me to go chopping up me own son, now!

Davey   Well, *I'm* not doing all the work! I'll tell you that!

Mairead   One of ye's chop up Padraic, the other be chopping the fella there with the cross in his gob. And don't be countermanding me orders, cos it's a fecking lieutenant ye're talking to now.

Davey (*to* **Donny**)   That sounds fairer, splitting the workload.

Donny   I suppose.

Mairead *collects up her rucksack and air rifle.*

Davey   Is it still off to the INLA you're going, Mairead?

Donny (*waving a hand at the carnage*)   Sure, there's no fecker left in the INLA now!

Mairead   No, David. I think I'll be staying around here for a biteen. I thought shooting fellas would be fun, but it's not. It's dull.

Davey   It gets boring easy.

Mairead   Aye.

Donny   Aye. Stick to cows.

Mairead *gives* **Donny** *an evil look.*

Donny (*scared*)   I'm upset over the death of me son, Mairead.

Mairead (*pause*)   I'm off home with Sir Roger. Be getting on with your chopping you two.

Davey   Aye.

Donny Aye.

They linger.

Mairead (*angrily*)   Be getting on, I'm saying! That's an order!

Donny *and* **Davey** *tut, kneel down and start hacking up the body parts again.*

Mairead   And it's an investigation tomorrow I'll be launching, when I've had a chance to think, about how Sir Roger came to end up in this house in the first place, and half black with it.

Donny *and* **Davey** *wince, their shoulders slumping, as they continue with their work.*

Mairead (*singing*)   'My only son was shot in Dublin, fighting for his country bold. He fought for Ireland and Ireland only. The harp and shamrock, green, white and gold.'

Mairead *exits. After they're sure she's gone,* **Donny** *and* **Davey** *stop work, still kneeling there, and hold their heads in their hands, groaning.*

Davey   Oh, will it never end? Will it never fecking end?

Donny   It fecking won't, d'you know!

Slight pause. A black cat scrambles through the hole high in the wall stage left and stands or walks along the shelf there. **Donny** *and* **Davey** *look at each other, then slowly turn and look at the cat.*

Davey   What the hell fecking cat is that, now?

Donny *gets up and goes over to it.*

Donny (*sickened*)   Fecking Wee fecking Thomas this fecking is!

Davey   No!

Donny   Aye!

Davey   How?

Donny   Off fecking gallivanting he must've been these two fecking days!

Davey   Off chasing fecking skirt!

Donny   Aye!

Davey *gets up and looks at the cat in* **Padraic***'s arms on the table.*

Davey   So who the feck is this fecking cat?

Donny   Some fecking stray that must've been, only looked like Wee Thomas.

Davey   So all this terror has been for absolutely nothing?

Donny   It has!

Davey   All because that fecker was after his hole? Four dead fellas, two dead cats . . . me hairstyle ruined! Have I missed anything?

Donny   Your sister broken-hearted.

Davey   Me sister broken-hearted.

Donny   All me shoe polish gone.

Davey   That cat deserves shooting!

Donny   He does, d'you know?

Davey *(pause. Thinking about it)*   He does, d'you know?

Davey *slowly turns and looks at the guns in* **Padraic***'s mouth. He waves a thumb at them. The two look at each other a moment, then go over and each pull a gun out of* **Padraic***.* **Donny** *picks the cat up off the shelf, or wherever he's got to, and places him on a clear spot on the table beside* **Padraic***. They both cock their guns and slowly raise them till they're pointed at the cat.*

Donny   But Davey . . . ?

Davey   What?

They lower their guns.

Donny   Hasn't there been enough killing done in this house for one day?

Davey (*pause*)   No.

Donny   One more won't fecking hurt!

They both aim their guns at the cat's head again, arms taut.

Donny   On a count of three, now.

Davey   Aye.

Both (*pause*)   One . . . (*Pause.*) Two . . . (*Pause.*) *Three!*

A long, long pause, arms taut, teeth gritted, not breathing. But neither of them can bring himself to do it.

Donny (*teeth gritted*)   Will we leave the poor beggar alone, Davey?

Davey (*teeth gritted*)   Will we, Donny?

Donny   We will!

Davey   We will!

The two breathe a sigh of relief, hearts pounding, slam the guns down on the table and stroke and pet the cat, trying to recover their breath.

Davey   There there, Wee Thomas. There there . . .

Donny *pours Wee Thomas some Frosties.*

Donny   There there, now, baby. Sure, you're home now. You're home now.

Davey   Home sweet home.

Donny   Home sweet home is right!

Fade to black as the cat eats the Frosties.

Donny   Didn't I tell you he likes Frosties, Davey?

[*If, however, the cat doesn't eat the Frosties, the above line should be substituted for:*

Davey   He doesn't like Frosties at all, Donny.]

Blackout.